MW00586977

*Catherine Ponder : The Dynamic
Laws of Prosperity Series*

Lesson 6

Giving makes you rich

All rights reserved. No part of this publication may be
reproduced, stored in a retrieval system, or
transmitted in any form or by any means, electronic,
mechanical, photocopying or otherwise, without the
prior permission of the copyright owner.

This book is a transcription of a series of lessons on
"The Dynamic Laws of Prosperity" by Catherine
Ponder.

© **Copyright 2006 – BN Publishing**

www.bnpublishing.com

info@bnpublishing.com

Transcription: Deena W.

ALL RIGHTS RESERVED

Printed in the U.S.A.

The Advanced Laws of

Prosperity

Now friends, the word "advanced", as we know, means to hasten. When you make great advances, you are hastening your good; you are hastening results. And so, the advanced laws of prosperity would be good laws that hasten results, those laws that hasten results. Now the advanced law of prosperity that hastens results is the prosperity secret that has been known simply as "giving and receiving". The advanced law of prosperity is that your giving makes you rich.

All right, we've already declared it, but let's declare it again: "My giving makes me rich". Together: "My giving makes me rich".

Now this isn't a new idea.

The ancient Egyptians, the Babylonians, the Persians, the Arabians, the Greeks, the Romans, even the Chinese, long before Biblical times, knew this idea; that giving can make us rich. They practiced this old, mystical success secret.

Now Abraham, whom I like to think of as the first millionaire of the Bible, Abraham learned this prosperity secret from the Babylonians. His grandson, Jacob, mentioned it as one of the success principles he planned to use when he left home, and started out to seek his fortune in a new land. Of course, Jacob did follow that success principle – the fact that he did follow it is obvious because he became one of the Bible's early millionaires.

Moses later emphasized this success principle and it was practiced by the Hebrews, who as we know, became one of the wealthiest groups the world has ever known. They credit much of their wealth over the centuries to their use of this prosperity idea; that our giving can make us rich.

Many of our modern millionaires have used this prosperity secret, and have often pointed it out as the formula that brought them riches. The list includes people like the Colgate people, the Hinsey suit people, the Kraft cheese people, the Rockefeller family. And so, our giving can make us rich, but only if we give in a certain way. Giving can make you rich when you give systematically. Systematic giving opens the way to systematic receiving, but when we do not give, we damn up, and stagnate, and close many channels to our good; we block them.

Now perhaps you're thinking: "Well, yes, but I do give. I give every cent I can to pay bills and to keep going financially". But that's enforced giving. You see, that isn't a free kind of giving. And so there is another kind of giving that we're thinking about in order to prosper. When we practice this other type of giving, putting it first in our financial affairs, then order comes into our financial affairs and to every phase of our world. We find ourselves being prospered in both expected and unexpected ways. Our money seems to go further. Other financial surprises come to us. Somehow, everything seems easier on a financial level.

Now the ancient people, who knew the wisdom of the ages, understood the nature of Universal Substance out of which all wealth comes. They knew that by consistently giving, you move on that Universal Substance; you form a vacuum which sets up, and then rushes in to fill with new supplies. That's the nature of Substance; it abhors a vacuum, and it rushes in to fill any vacuum. And so giving, in order to make way to receive, is a scientific method that works to prosper those who use it consistently.

Now, this is a giving Universe; we have to give constantly in order to receive constantly, because the Universe is constantly giving to us. If we do not balance the act of receiving by giving in some good and happy way, in a free sense, voluntarily, then the Universe seems to force us to give anyway, in unhappy ways. But give we must, because it is the law of the Universe. And so the Universal law: "Give and it shall be given unto you", works whether we want it too, or not.

Where there is no voluntary giving, something is taken from us. People who think that they cannot afford to give constructively and freely have to give anyway – destructively and involuntarily. They are the ones who have to give to the doctors and the hospitals for their ill health; they have to give to the lawyers for their accidents, for their legal and business problems; they have to give to accountants and to Internal Revenue for their income tax problems, and in many undesirable, and in many unhappy ways.

What!

And so, if you do not give voluntarily of your financial resources, you can expect the Substance of the Universe to get damned up in your affairs. If you do not give voluntarily of your financial resources, you can expect that bodily ailment, financial entanglement, human relations problems and general confusion will follow in your affairs.

Work

Now, when you see a person who has constant problems of all kinds; when you see a person who has constant problems of ill health, financial difficulties, family inharmony, general confusion, and dissatisfaction in their lives, not only are they not thinking right and not talking right, but they're not giving right, either. And so where there is no voluntary giving, something is taken from them anyway.

We cannot cheat the basic law of the Universe, which is giving and receiving. It works regardless of our mis-working it. We can only cheat ourselves out of much health, wealth and happiness by trying to bypass it, or by bypassing it. Someone has called this great law of life "the great law of give and take". Give, and then take; claim your good, you see. And so how can we practice the other type of giving, giving constructively so as to avoid having to give destructively?

Well, the ancient people believed that the number "10" was the magic number of increase. They invoked this magic number by regularly giving one-tenth of all channels of their income to their leaders, their religious leaders that preached to their tabernacle and to their temple. Now, the Hebrews were required to give a tenth of all channels of income for these purposes, and this included giving a tenth of everything – their gold, their silver, their jewels, their cattle, sheep, flocks, a tenth of fruit, grain, all crops, financial income and assets of all types, because they felt that this was a Universal law.

Now, the first instance of tithing recorded in the Bible occurred when Abraham gave his tithes to the Priest of Salem, and it's so interesting that after Abraham had given that tithe, he was made a very interesting promise: a promise of riches and prosperity; a promise of protection from the negative experiences of life. The Lord said: "I am thy shield and thy exceeding great reward". " I am thy shield" - I will protect you from the negative experiences of life, and I am "thy exceeding great reward" - I will prosper you abundantly. Not a little bit - "exceeding great reward". It's a marvelous prosperity promise for anyone who uses this same prosperity law today.

And so "10" is still the magic number of increase. Now to help remind you of the power of that number 10, we have placed in your prosperity kit the little card that says: "10, the magic number of increase". And so it's just a reminder of this marvelous, old, prosperity law. "10" is still the magic number of increase.

And so let's declare it: "10 is still the magic number of increase". Together: "10 is still the magic number of increase". Good.

One of the wealthiest men who ever lived, of course, was Solomon, and he made an interesting prosperity promise too, when he said: "Honor the Lord with thy substance and with the first fruits of thine increase; so shall thy barns be filled with plenty, and thy vats shall overflow with new wine". Again, there's abundance, you see. We weren't promised just a little bit. "Thy barns shall be filled with plenty, and thy vats shall overflow" - overflow with wine.

And so, this is really one of the laws of prosperity, the laws of abundance. It is the advanced law; it is the law that advances, or hastens, or steps-up our good.

Now the idea, the story that has meant so much to me, and the story that started me tithing many years ago, at a time when I couldn't afford to tithe, but I couldn't afford not to either because I needed the prosperity law to work for me in a wonderful way – and so, if you'll take the little booklet, "As You Tithe, So You Prosper", and look at page 40 – and I love this story, at the bottom of page 40:

"He who said he found it necessary to tithe in order to get

out of debt, voiced a truth that has become as evident to thousands. A man who was $10,000 in debt with his credit company, and a wife and 4 children for whom to provide, took a position as a day laborer in a mill, and with his family was compelled to live in a tent. He met two Divinity students, who convinced him that he should tithe. The same week that he began tithing, the company offered him one of its houses in which to live; within a year, he was promoted to foreman; 10 years later, he was free from debt, the owner of a large lumber company, owner of his own home which was large and beautifully furnished, and of a large car; also an airplane and other things on a similar scale. He attributes his success to first recognizing his debt to God, and faithfully tithing of his income.

Tithing establishes order in our mind, body, and affairs. When order exists, we cannot remain in debt. He who first begins to tithe while in debt, invariably reports later that he is free from debt."

Now you will love this little book, because it has so many marvelous prosperity stories in it. I like the story that the lady told me in Southern California about learning how she could tithe her way to prosperity. She and her husband had seven growing children for whom they were struggling financially, even though her husband worked for one of the major television studios on the Coast. And so, after she learned that 10 was the magic number of increase, she decided to try it. She began to tithe from their current income, and soon an opportunity opened for some of her children to appear in television commercials. For this they were well paid. As they tithed from this income, the way opened then for all of her children to do television commercials, from which they received handsome residuals. They continued to tithe from all channels of income, and within 2 years, this family had moved into a $60,000 home, which to them seemed like really a dream house. The husband had a better job, all of the seven children were working in their spare time on television, trust funds were set up for their education, and now their future seems assured financially.

A friend said to this woman, "Doing television commercials is such competitive work, that I don't see how your children have done so well. The average actor feels lucky to get 2 or 3 jobs a year doing commercials, yet your children have appeared in 30 commercials this past year!" And this woman said, "10 is the magic number of increase. We tithe all channels of income, so it isn't strange that our children would receive 10 times as much work as those actors who do not tithe. This is the prosperity law."

Now, it's an interesting thing to me, friends, that the act of tithing, or of giving a tenth of one's income back to the Universe, through God's work, is not something that some minister dreamed up as a means of getting money out of people. Instead, it is a Universal prosperity law, practiced down through the centuries as a method of prospering people on a permanent basis. When you give consistently, you open the way to receive consistently.

Many people have had a psychological block about tithing, and rightly so, because so many well-meaning theologians who were too zealous have stressed what tithing could do for the Temple, rather than what it could do for the individual. When you look up the great tithing promises in the Bible that are so famous, you find that the Bible says that the individual who tithes will be prosperous. Of course, it goes without saying that his church will be prosperous too, but that is secondary, and not the prime cause of tithing. As Eli Myer has said: "As you tithe, so you prosper".

Sometimes people say, "But I cannot afford to tithe", and of course that is the time when we cannot afford not to. The greater the present financial necessity, the greater the need for immediately invoking: "10, the magic number of increase", so as to increase our prosperity.

You can attempt this idea of tithing in small ways first, just to prove it to your own satisfaction, if you wish. A businesswoman was in a financial bind. She had moved from one part of the country to another, she had gone into a new line of work; it was paying off, but not fast enough to meet her expenses. She practiced all of the laws of prosperity in an effort to demonstrate immediate cash. Nothing seemed to work for her, though, until she suddenly remembered that she had gotten careless about her tithing. She sat down and wrote out a tithe of the money that she had on hand; she had $500 left, and so she wrote out the tithe for $50 and immediately put it in the mail to her church. Now, the interesting thing was that the next day, she began to get calls for work that tided her over financially; but nothing happened until she tithed first.

And so, it's an interesting idea that "10" is the magic number of increase. Now, one of the stories that I like to tell, and you will recall it from one of the books, is about the man who went from rags to riches after the age of 50 through tithing. This was a man who had never found his true place in life; this was a man who had gotten rather disenchanted with churches and with religion, and had spent every Sunday on the golf course for many years. One night, he and his wife attended a prosperity lecture such as this, and heard about this idea of tithing, and it made sense to him. He could see that it was scientific, that it was orderly, that it was business-like, that it was professional. Consistent giving would open the way to consistent receiving, and so he decided to try it.

Now at this particular point in his life, this man, being past the age of 50, was driving an old car, he was living in a rented house, he was wearing threadbare clothes, his wife was in ill health, and they were spending every cent they had trying to get her healed. And so, this man decided to try this idea, reasoning that he would rather share a tenth of his income with that church where he had learned this idea, rather than spend many times that amount for negative and unwanted experiences in life such as he had had for 50 years. And so, as he began to tithe, he expected good things to happen; he expected to be prospered and protected, and he was.

The first thing that happened was that he was able to get a job that he liked as an agent for a steel company, as a sales agent for a steel company. The next thing that happened, he noticed, was that his wife's health began to improve; they had less and less medical expense. Then his income began to rise, as he became an expert at selling his company's product. Within 2 years, his employer passed away and the local dealership of this steel company was available. This man said that since he was tithing and expecting to be prospered and protected, that he had the courage to go to his banker and ask for a loan. He said if he had not been tithing, he wouldn't have had the courage to do it, because it seemed like a rather large financial undertaking.

Now, as he began to continue to tithe, his business, which he had now bought, began to prosper even more, and from that point on his success increased by leaps and bounds. Soon he was able to start an investment program for himself and his family, and when

I first met this man about 15 years ago, he was financially independent. When people say to him, "What happened? For so many years I knew you, and you were really a failure; and then all of the sudden you blossomed forth. What happened?" And he always says: "I tithed my way to prosperity."

He made an interesting statement one time. He said: "From the day that I began to tithe, I have never hesitated to buy anything I wanted, or to do anything I wished to do. I have felt that since

I was sharing my substance with the Universe, I could expect to be prospered, guided, and protected in all that I undertook, and I have been". Now he's become financially independent, and he's done it in a rather easy way. He's now semi-retired, he travels around the world, he plays golf and bridge, and so on, and has a marvelous time.

All right. As the little card says, why strain and strive when you can tithe and thrive? And so, let's turn it into prosperity jingle: "I no longer strain and strive, I tithe and thrive". Let's declare it together: "I no longer strain and strive, I tithe and thrive". Good.

I once knew 2 professional men who were partners. One tithed, and the other one didn't, and it was very interesting to watch what happened. The man who did not tithe made $20,000 a year at that period; he made the most, the other man only made $12,000 a year. The one who did not tithe made $20,000 a year; he worked night and day and weekends in an effort to make ends meet, but he could barely get by financially.

There were frequent spells of illness and unexpected mishaps in his family that were always causing unexpected expense. The harder he worked, the harder he had to work. Paying the bills was a constant struggle; collecting money from his clients was difficult, too.

His business associate only made $12,000 a year, but he tithed. He and his family lived much better. They had a nicer home, they resided in a better neighborhood, they always seemed to have more, they certainly enjoyed life more;

they did not have the illnesses, the accidents, the extra expense that the first family did. This man never thought of working nights or weekends. His clients liked him and paid their accounts on time. After several years, he left his associate and went into business for himself. Soon he was making a great deal more money than his former associate was making, and he was still enjoying life more, too. And so, somehow, by tithing, he seemed to be prospered and protected in return.

In loosening our purse strings, we loosen many other things that have bound us in life. In loosening our purse strings, we seem to loosen many negative, unhappy, unnecessary, unwanted experiences in life. We find that we begin to feel freer, and one of the things that we seem to free in the process is our many, many problems. Now sometimes people say, "Well, I do not tithe regularly, but I give large sums occasionally." It does more good to tithe regularly smaller amounts than to give larger amounts sporadically. Just as it is necessary to breathe out regularly in order to receive fresh air into the lungs, it is necessary to give regularly if you wish to receive regularly.

A wealthy lady heard a lecture on tithing, and though she and her husband had given substantial donations to their church, they had never given consistently, and they had never tithed. Even though their yearly income seemed sizeable, there was never enough money on hand to meet many private needs after they paid their income taxes. Much of their money went back into their business, and so, in spite of having several channels of income, this wealthy woman always felt financially limited. She decided that the fault might be in her lack of consistent giving through tithing; and so, after beginning to tithe, she said that she felt a sense of security, and satisfaction, and peace of mind about her financial affairs for the first time.

Within a few months, she received a long distance call one day from the manager of one of her farms in another State. He said, "For the first time in years, the farm has recently made some money. There is now $10,000 available in profits from the farm. What do you want me to do with the money?" This lady said that previously, it would have been necessary for her to consider the matter for some time, before knowing what to do with that $10,000, but as she talked to her manager by long distance, she said that it just flashed to her how to invest the money; how to reinvest it in farm supplies, equipment, seeds for the next year's crops, and so on. Her guidance later proved to be very good. Soon her farm was making more money than at any previous period.

Now, as she continued to tithe, her husband raised her private allowance, a relative started sending her gifts of $3000 – this was back in the days when, you know, you could give away $3000, I think it's $6000 now, to relatives, rather than leaving in a will later; it has to do with the tax laws of inheritance. And so, this lady began to get these $3000 checks at regular intervals from a relative who had never given her anything before. And she said later that everything in her financial affairs began to smooth out, and she began to really feel prosperous for the first time in her life, as a certain sense of freedom and circulation took place.

Now, a woman said one time, "I don't see why I should tithe my money, because I tithe my time; I'm a Sunday school teacher." And I said, "Well, that's fine. All ministers and churches love Sunday school teachers, but what are you trying to demonstrate: more time or more money?" And she said, "Well, I would like to have more time, but I certainly need more money." Now I suggested that she check out the tithing promises in the Bible, because they all speak of tithing money and financial assets; they do not talk about tithing one's time, although that's a notable thing to do.

Now, a woman in Florida heard about tithing, and decided to begin to tithe from her small retirement income, and immediately after she began to tithe from her small retirement income, she was offered a part-time job and accepted it. Then she realized that the Bible talks about tithing a tenth of everything, and this began to bother her because she had a savings account with $5,000 in it. She decided that tithing a tenth of everything meant tithing a tenth of all of her financial assets, and so she decided to tithe from that savings account. She drew out $500 from savings, she gave it to the church where she had learned this idea, and in a few days she heard from the local Social Security Board. They asked her to come in and see them, and at first she was worried. Her first reaction was, "Now what have I done wrong?" And so upon visiting the Social Security Board she was rather apologetic, she said, "Well, I, I'm receiving my social security check every month, thank you". And they said, "Well, we owe you an apology", they said, "We owe you some money; because of a new government regulation, the fact that you were born before a certain date means that we owe you $1250". And she said, "Mrs.

Ponder, I couldn't talk those people out of giving me that $1250!" And so, it was a very interesting idea, you see, after she had tithed the $500, then it came right back to her, multiplied. This often happens.

Another tither said that she had always wondered why her savings account did not seem to grow. First she would put money in it, and then she would take money out of it. Finally, it dawned on her that she was not tithing from the interest income on that account, though she tithed from other channels of supply. As she began tithing on the interest income, her savings began to grow steadily.

And then, a businessman was worried because his investments did not seem to prosper him as they should. He said that he began to realize that he was tithing from other channels of income, but that he had never tithed from his stocks or from his stock income; and so, after tithing from his stock income, he said that he began to gain certain feelings and certain guidance about certain stocks that he should sell, others in which he should invest, that brought him a far, more handsome income.

Most of us know the story of the famous engineering genius who became a multi-millionaire through the tithing idea, Robert LeTourneau. I imagine that some of our business professional men here have read his book, "Mover of Men and Mountains", in which he speaks of the time after he started tithing. When business got so good that one year he decided to hold on to the tithes, and so he had a little conversation with his creator, and he said: "God, we've had a great year, you and I. And so instead of giving you your tithe of $100,000 which the business owes you this year, I'm going to do you a favor. I'm going to reinvest that $100,000 in business, and you will get that tithe and much more next year." He said that he suffered one financial reverse after another. Bad weather kept his construction work from going forward; at the end of the year it was very interesting that he was exactly $100,000 in debt.

He learned from that experience never to withhold the tithes, never to try to bargain with God about it. And then, in reflecting upon $100,000 lesson that he learned, he made a little quip. He said, "It's all right to give God credit for our success, but He can also use cash." Now of course, as you know, his tithes later ran into the millions of dollars, and he had to form a private foundation just to handle the distribution of them.

A salesman once had prospered so much through tithing that he was trying to convince everyone he knew that it was a great prosperity law, and he wanted to know what to say to the owner of his company. A friend suggested that he remind his boss that many of this country's millionaires attribute their wealth to tithing, that tithing is a tried and true method in business.

O.K/True

Now it's also important where
you give. You should give at the
point or points where you are
receiving spiritual help and
inspiration. For instance, a
woman said, "I have some
apartment that I cannot keep
rented, and I use all the prosperity
laws you talk about; and don't tell
me to tithe, because I'm already
tithing." And so I said to her,
"Where are you tithing?" She
said, " I cannot see that it matters
where I tithe, so I tithe to the
church that I used to attend,
because they keep sending me

bills." But she said, "I no longer attend that church because I get my inspiration by elsewhere, at another temple." And so of course, the answer was: tithe where you're getting your help and inspiration. If you wish to be prosperous, it is inconsistent to do otherwise.

To get help from one place, and to give to another, is like going to one doctor for help and trying to pay another; it's like eating in one restaurant but trying to pay for it in another – it's inconsistent. Give where you are receiving spiritual help and inspiration. This keeps you in touch with the flow of supply. Now the marvelous thing about the tithing idea, of course, is that if we are receiving help and inspiration from several channels, then we have plenty to give in several ways, you see. Our giving really makes us feel rich.

A woman started tithing for financial reasons and was prospered, but she said that she had a surprise. For years, she had tried to lose weight and had been unable to do so. She said that when she started tithing, not only was she prospered, but that she immediately tithed away 15 pounds! So, now here's a new idea for the weight situation. Tithing helps free us from the negative experiences of life.

A woman who is now in the millionaire bracket said, "When something negative happens to me, I know I haven't given enough; a negative experience is always an indication to me to give. I always say, what do I need to give, and I give it."

Someone has said, there is one basic problem in life – congestion; there is one basic solution – circulation. And so, if your financial affairs have stagnated into indebtedness, or hard times, or constant problems, or confusion, you can clear up the congestion, begin to clear the channels, you can get the law of circulation working in your affairs again, through the act of consistent giving, through the act of consistent tithing, returning to the Universe a portion of that which the Universe has given to you.

A man in the real estate business in Southern California said that he learned quite a lesson about giving, and about careless giving. He said that he got careless in the distribution of his tithes one month when he gave a relative – a problem pronged relative – his tithes, rather than giving it impersonally to his church, and he said everything went wrong. His bank account got mixed up, a number of checks bounced, a real estate deal from which he expected a commission of several thousand dollars did not go through, other channels of supply simply dried up, and he was left in a financial bind. Everything stagnated until he again began to tithe impersonally.

Now, there's nothing wrong in giving to people in need if we're careful what we give them; but by giving only money, we offer only temporary help to people who are in need, and therefore we keep them in poverty. It's far wiser to give them literature or ideas on how they can begin to prosper themselves. This helps to prosper them permanently; it makes them independent of handouts.

The ancient laws on tithing were very definite about where we should give. The ancient laws on tithing said this: that the first tenth went to the place of worship, or to the place where you received help spiritually. The first tenth went to the place of worship. This tithe was given impersonally; the giver had nothing to say about how it was to be spent. The second tithe — because of course the people of the Old Testament gave several tithes - the second tithe was a festival tithe; the third tithe was a charity tithe. And so, if you're giving several tithes, several tenths of your income – and of course internal revenue now allows you up to 50% as a tax write-off – and so if you're giving several tenths of your income, rather than only one tenth, perhaps you may feel freer about your second or third tenth, but your first tenth should be given impersonally, with no stipulation as to how it is to be used.

Now, if you are not free to tithe
from all channels of supply, start
tithing from one channel. Test this
tithing idea in some way, quietly
and privately. One businessman
said that when he began to tithe a
tenth of something, that that was
the turning point in his career.

Everything took an upswing. And
so, if you're not free to tithe from
all channels of supply, or aren't
yet convinced that you should,
then test the idea by tithing from
one channel of supply. If you do
not yet feel guided to tithe gross,

then tithe net, but begin using "10, the magic number of increase" in some way, and you will begin to prove the power of it for yourself.

A businessman in Detroit began tithing and he said that he had a surprise. He was immediately relieved of a job that he didn't really like of longstanding. This man then continued to tithe from his unemployment checks. As he continued to tithe, he went on to a $20,000 a year job from which he continued tithing. Now, at the time that he tithed from his unemployment check, after he had lost the job he didn't like anyway, he also was enduring an unhappy marriage, and that dissolved. He said that he found that tithing straightened out every phase of his life. He said to a friend, "When I began to tithe, limitation turned me loose." And so, it's an interesting idea how it can work on all levels of life.

Now friends, in closing I would like to remind you that "10" is the magic number of increase; that this is one of the ways to invoke the laws of prosperity. Now, we do not have them in our kit for you, but if you are interested in using the tithing idea right away, we do have the tithe envelopes available. They are at a table at the back. Sometimes at the close of seminars, people like to immediately use these ideas, and so you'll find them there along with other information that may be of interest to you. Sometimes people like to send in checks later, just to prove this idea, right away. In any event, let us declare:

"I no longer strain and strive, I tithe and thrive." Together: "I no longer strain and strive, I tithe and thrive." "I tithe my way to prosperity." Together: "I tithe my way to prosperity." "My giving makes me rich." "My giving makes me rich."

All right, this is it. These are the dynamic laws of prosperity.

THE END

We suggest you now read the book,

"Automatic Wealth, the Secrets of the Millionaire Mind-Including: As a Man Thinketh, the Science of Getting Rich, the Way to Wealth & Think and Grow Rich [UNABRIDGED] (Paperback) by Napoleon Hill, James Allen, Wallace D. Wattles, Benjamin Franklin[1] " carefully.

---

1   Available at   www.bnpublishing.com

We hope that after you have the opportunity to practice the principles involved in these lessons, you will write to us and let us know of the results in your life[2].

BN Publishing

Improving People's Life

www.bnpublishing.com

---

2   info@bnpublishing.com

BN Publishing

Improving People's Life

www.bnpublishing.com

We have Book Recommendations for you

The Strangest Secret by Earl Nightingale
(Audio CD - Jan 2006)

Acres of Diamonds [MP3 AUDIO]
[UNABRIDGED] (Audio CD) by Russell H.
Conwell

Automatic Wealth: The Secrets of the
Millionaire Mind--Including: Acres of
Diamonds, As a Man Thinketh, I Dare you!,
The Science of Getting Rich, The Way to
Wealth, and Think and Grow Rich
[UNABRIDGED]
by Napoleon Hill, et al (CD-ROM)

Think and Grow Rich [MP3 AUDIO]
[UNABRIDGED]
by Napoleon Hill, Jason McCoy (Narrator)
(Audio CD - January 30, 2006)

As a Man Thinketh [UNABRIDGED]
by James Allen, Jason McCoy (Narrator)
(Audio CD)

Your Invisible Power: How to Attain Your
Desires by Letting Your Subconscious Mind
Work for You [MP3 AUDIO]
[UNABRIDGED]
by Genevieve Behrend, Jason McCoy
(Narrator) (Audio CD)

Thought Vibration or the Law of Attraction
in the Thought World [MP3 AUDIO]
[UNABRIDGED]
by William Walker Atkinson, Jason McCoy
(Narrator) (Audio CD - July 1, 2005)

The Law of Success Volume I: The
Principles of Self-Mastery by Napoleon Hill
(Audio CD - Feb 21, 2006)

The Law of Success, Volume I: The
Principles of Self-Mastery (Law of Success,
Vol 1) (The Law of Success) by Napoleon
Hill (Paperback - Jun 20, 2006)

The Law of Success , Volume II & III: A
Definite Chief Aim & Self Confidence by
Napoleon Hill (Paperback - Jun 20, 2006)

**Thought Vibration or the Law of Attraction
in the Thought World & Your Invisible
Power (Paperback)**

**Automatic Wealth, The Secrets of the
Millionaire Mind-Including:As a Man
Thinketh, The Science of Getting Rich, The
Way to Wealth and Think and Grow Rich
(Paperback)**

The Bestsellers on this Book give sound advice
about money or how to obtain it. Just shoot to
the stars and stay focused on your dreams and it
will happen. There is nothing that we can
imagine, that we can't do. So what are we
waiting for, let's begin the journey of self
fullfillment.

4 Bestsellers in 1 Book:

As a Man Thinketh by James Allen

The Science of Getting Rich by Wallace D. Wattles

The Way to Wealth by Benjamin Franklin

Think and Grow Rich by Napoleon Hill

Get Published!

BN Publishing helped authors publish more titles. So whether you're writing a romance novel, historical fiction, mystery, action and suspense, poetry, children's or any other genre, we can help you reach your publishing goals.

Paperback

Reach 20,000 retail accounts in the U.S. (including chains, independents, specialty stories, and libraries).

Including:

www.amazon.com

www.amazon.co.uk

www.amazon.ca

www.bn.com

www.powells.com

www.ebay.com

and more...

Your book will be included in a physical catalog that will go out to over 20,000 retail stores.

When your title is entered into our library it will automatically appear in the bookstore and library databases.

Our United States and United Kingdom based sales teams works with publisher clients based throughout the world who want to print books in the United States and United Kingdom, or reach the North American, UK and wider European markets through our broad distribution channel partners.

If we decide to publish it:

we will send you 2 free copies of the finished book;

we will give you 10% royalty of the selling price of each book copy sold (selling price = the price the book is sold by BN Publishing to wholesalers or other resellers);

and if you wish to have more copies of your book, we will sell you the book for two thirds of the list price.

Please send us more information about your book to info@bnpublishing.com

BN Publishing

Improving People's Life

www.bnpublishing.com

BN Publishing

Improving People's Life

www.bnpublishing.com

Printed in the United States
108421LV00006B/3/A